THE FIRST THIRTY YEARS EP

Adam Barrett is a poet and novelist from the North East of England. His poems have been published across anthologies, zines, online magazines and journals. Adam's work is inspired by class, masculinity, history, punk culture and the North East landscape. *The First Thirty Years EP* is his debut pamphlet. He was the recipient of the Sid Chaplin Award at the 2024 Northern Writers' Awards for his novel in progress.

ISBN: 978-1-917617-25-3

The author has asserted their right to be identified as the author of this Work in accordance with the Copyright, Designs and Patents Act 1988

Cover designed by Aaron Kent

Edited and Typeset by Aaron Kent

Broken Sleep Books Ltd
PO BOX 102
Llandysul
SA44 9BG

CONTENTS

The First Thirty Years EP

Adam Barrett

Broken Sleep Books

IN GOD'S BLIND EYE

Between ripples of autumn dates,
Durham stills in the Wear's glass.

A millennium's window fragments
the cathedral, pieces it together

in a smoking breath.
Where sheer banks of the choked

peninsula protect the saint and Bede,
the innocent have been failed.

A stone's throw from God's hand,
they were silenced.

Where the water darkens beyond
marching miners, you saw your reflection,

murky and breaking beneath that Green Bridge.

MAN UP

Carve MAN UP into your chest
reversed to reflect true

a mirror's reminder
to let blood pool and thicken,

set another layer to your skin, or at least

to look manly
to gain credit you need to feel

you belong.

WHAT IS OURS

Within those flowing hills and rugged coast
communities cement themselves into history:
reigning champions of child poverty and suicide.
For the hills and coast stretch far beyond the line
where the House begins to care;
their bloodlines cared, they might remember,
for by this coast and in these hills
they built their industries,
and in those industries, our bloodlines worked,
choked and died before fifty. Mined, built, crafted ships
with their bare hands and formed connections with the world,
for an Empire to plunder and pillage and call it protection.
But in our hills and by our coast,
character blooms infinitely.

ENGLAND

England is a Molotov
a billionaire's oil
in its ale bottles,
fused with tabloids, lit
with flames pillaged
from indigenous peoples.

RED-BRICK TALES

You are the violence, the pebble-dashed terraces said.
You're the flag-from-a-window, postcode-pride,
what's-this-country-becoming type, so say it so.
You're nettles casting slabs aside, caning
the hanging ankles of backer-riders. No stopping for docks —
there's manning-up to do. Fences won't hop themselves to reach
unplayable pitches, where pit-bike tracks have sliced
the six-yard box and glass decorates goal lines like the salt
frozen beneath fingernails.

On the beach you abseil the cliffs to reach,
you stuff those hands into tracksuit pockets —
they could think the salt is glitter.
Foam whispers lullabies at your feet as your back finds the cliff face,
taunting dusk. You were never trapped for the reasons you thought
but trapped by the place they fold their lips at and feign intrigue.
Dilute future words, stare at your mouth
and consider the shape of theirs — that's your legacy,
stretched vowels and not a word you write.
Safety boots and opposing stripes,
the same despite the differences.

CRUMBLING

The passing Summer Solstice
draws an emptiness

an urge to give up on the warmth and build
for the coming cold,

but in lingering heat,
off-white walls begin t o   crack
fr   om   skirting up,
dis   located   fingers clut ching   roots

like bouquets of   dying flowers

                    in fists

of spouses-to-be   never married.

First dust,
                    flaking plaster,
   sheets and slabs
of brick and stone.

Wires
   re
    pel

and

coil aboutmythroat
hidden pythons liberated
from claustrophobia,

the prison cell
between In and Out.

WE ARE THE RATS

Refuse to scurry under the authority of night —
it's better to die by our own flames,
than choke on their poison.
If we'd seen beyond innocent lenses,
as we lit fires below naked canopies,
would we have waited
to burn the world down?

TAKING CHASE

Late August peeled from beach chalets with the dry skin flaked
    from collarbones.
You dreamt of love before your time, exaggerated
the glint in passing eyes that you know was your reflection.
Balloons of carbon, smooth-skinned and featureless,
bobbing to the gentle release of long nights
and songs you can't relate to.
You searched for the place where you wanted to decay
and still to find it. Somewhere with trees and hills forever
where animals graze with no use-by date, where the rain feeds
and the sun wakes, where the nights are black and the mornings pink.
Drowsy light trickles down the crag, a waterfall of grapefruit
igniting the golf balls to meteor showers,
raining upon dog-walkers, and the bucket-suckers hidden
in their manhunt dens, carpets furnished with White Ace
and balls of foil and ash. You're ready to take chase,
geared for the thrill of running down the hillside,
obstructed by trees and laughter, tackled by stitches
and breathlessness and the sound of your persecutor.

AN OLD ME I STILL HATE

Shuffled through swelling heartache
in a club you hated

music with no meaning
a BPM to match the panic.

Exaggerated laughter cuts
through interludes of silence.

A passing smile from a girl you don't know
and a sip of something blue

churns a cocktail in your gut.
You leave with the same smile

you manage twice a week,
as streetlights dissolve and you're left

with abstract patterns of gold
thrown across the roads

from takeaways and after parties.
You take to allies to escape

the fights and pleas for floors to crash,
you wander on the main road, stop to piss

into the wind and spit hot bile on shoes
not quite paid off.

You can't do this forever, but
you can do it long enough to rot.

FROZEN IN THE VALLEY

Winter sets into the spine
as loam harmonies rise,
stirring a warmth to feed the buried
giants separated by the river.
The womb beneath the soil births
fungi for only the trained eye.

Derwent spits fog:
a bush viper, beautiful and wild,
pines breath caught in the bitterness,
ascending the village to fairy tale status.
There's fra reason to live,
few to leave,
yet we dwell on the money and the light
and the lack of it all.

THE WATER'S DIVIDE

See a lunar mass rise,
arch and pull away Trace
the gradient and its meandering
tail – does the coastal roar
still set its path?

Find the eye and the mill,
changing with the world –
do they still honour time
as they promised?

LOOKING FOR THE OSPREY

Palms aloft to feed the tributaries,
the snare beckons the first fall —
it comes a weighted blanket,
warm against burnt limbs.
The osprey does not answer.
Yarrow dances with the bend,
peppering angelic glitter over patches
of wild and tarmac open to the elements.
Thick lines of ancient soil adorn our cheeks
and foreheads in uneven arrows,
war paint for a culmination of centuries.
Towers of black pine soldiers stand silhouetted on the ridge,
they march into the travelling rain as it drags its ragged form
over county lines like the parting wool over North Pennines yonder.
At the break of cloud and hush over the reservoir,
the osprey does not answer.

THIRTY

Thirty was the destination. A bus replacement found nineteen.
Cold office and cabinets of cases to cycle through before
they're shredded — is that the cure?
Sertraline bump and peaty chaser, double positive
or rendered mute?

Placebo for pharmaceutical profit or elixir to add the years?

Adds perspective to the rope: still, despite the battering wind
strangling a timeless oak, above a deliberate path and ducked
below daily.

Is that a swing?
Not sure, son. Could be.

Some become familiar with its grip
Some experiment with serotonin
and the rest wonder what the hell it's all about.

The choice to empathise or criticise - selfish act or only way out?

Their poor mothers. Only 30. Tragic. 29. Even worse. 45. Scraping
the data line. 55. Not too bad. Nearly home time, anyway.

Who made the decision to take the body and leave the rope?

A reminder

A warning

A temptation

FOUR CHURCHES

A

jutting ridge

of green cloaks the first.

It's spire peers above the trees I can't identify.

Stone spirals where I expect a lonely window to house

an imprisoned heir, alas it's only capped by summer's dust.
Undisturbed by the bypass.

The second is a slab of brick, leaning as if dropped from the sky.
Red and sturdy, reducing terraces to scattered teeth of a broken jaw.
But for one minute a day, the clock no longer works, but still the
Sunday stream trickle in on time.

The third's façade is non-descript. House of God or abandoned post
office. It has no spire nor impressive door, nor glass set in colour. It
appears akin to labour movements and hidden revolutionaries than
holy matters.

The fourth is now a shell. Decrepit and dying, leaking the last of its
memories to the surrounding believers, who now walk further to
the post office. The fourth's windows crack in the corners, its doors
engraved with drawings only teenagers can do justice, graffitied by
hearts with initials chiselled out.

By the roadside, aligning with the central arch of three, stands a
lamppost. Cable-tied to it is a single bouquet stripped of life, the
corresponding note claimed by the wicked impartiality of wind.

I leave the fourth behind, and I am home.

VICTIM COMPLEX

Master of the written word,
what words could you conjure from that beacon?
A shaking prayer, screamed or choked on the salt
that cut the creases in your brow.

A gnarled hand found your blue mouth.
Choral waves kissed the approaching vessels.
His infinite garden, inherited from God and godly men,
claimed by an unnatural horde.

The wind ordered you to flee,
flee from the sea serpents breaking in the wash.
Flee from the *whirlwinds*
Flashes of lightning
Fiery dragons.
Cry to fellow men and Heaven
before your blood marbles with the sea,
before the priory is a house of unholy rot,
before the island feeds on your flesh,
Flee.

A millennium passes and more.

We stand where you did, our sentences peppered,
with words his killers gave us,
our tourists flitting between landmarks of our invaders.

I wonder what every nation we claimed
think when they look out at sea.

I see them flood from the train in the county,
That revolutionised it, the county whose ownership was stolen
Who turned the wheels of the world and pushed the ships to sea -
the same sea they sold

It took the region to bring tears:
Our commonality, an extra beat, scarlet receding with the hill.
A hole in the trees opened a window to the spires and
a tunnel for the river's breeze to cool an unexpected late-
September warmth.

A snap, then silence as they see it.
Its beauty is theirs too if they know its story.
Yes, of kings and queens, bishops and lords,
but the tale of stone and callused palms, buried names, our reach
into the sea
and the points we admire it from.

THE DAY WE LOST THE SUN WAR

in the end we're hunter-gatherers, foraging
sun shards beneath the desolation

on borderless plains of unowned land
the earth is turned without fuel

by scratch and scrape ashen slivers
surface like promising seedlings

frail and bled of warmth collected
with every era, we piece

fragments of solar heritage
we never got to share

THE GALA

Crimson gold whip from the Wear. If windless they'd dance on spirit of the core, souls lifted from firedamp clouds beneath our emerald land. Remember the kings and emperors of the Saxon North, the monks and their island slaughter, but save your wonder for the trappers stopped in their youth and their survivors – by fifty they knew four decades Below. Remember the grinding bone, the cartilage tying generations and the fights of fists and thought to keep our connections connected.

NIGHTS IN SHIELDS

The bairns still splutter at its salt,
dust their feet at the roadside.
Perched
trembling
Faces contorting brain-freeze,
smiling beneath hooded towels,
cones leaking into buckets of rock pools
their parents don't want to take home
but carry anyway.
The lilo he insisted on, tucked below his arm -
she told him to deflate it, but he'll carry it to win.
She'll overrule at the car. She knows he has the keys
and he has no memory.
Neon livens the strip,
fish and chips here
school holiday deal
freshly caught last month.
They'll wander through the haze
of salt and frying oil, and they'll spend
a day's wage on paper tickets for two-pence coins.
The only time those bairns will see that coin.
A couple trek the dunes barefoot.

Crawling   running

Crawling   running
Crawling   running

Crawling   running

They race, stop to gather a dropped shoe, race,
stop to cuddle, race, stop to wrestle,
end in a kiss.

Fuchsia soaks the caravans
running parallel to the closing tide
and early smell of surfer barbecues.
Flames and bottles popping to the set
from the fairground DJ —
it's not Ibiza, but
it's home.

NORTH SEA FROM A DISTANCE

Birdsong mounts camp from the Mouth –
odd to feel its warmth. Lilac breaks the day
beyond the warehouse, swallows the shooting
range with pre-dawn beads a haze in their wake.
The beeps and rumbles and podcast voices roll
between the ears as we meet morning, and we fear
for a second, uniforms fighting through the lilac
and the haze, crossing the road of broken workers
in their broken cars and gunning us down.

Our bones to rest by those charred in blackdamp
pockets, the insulation between coal walls.
Smog-stained and littered with ashen scars above
each serpentine divide, sea clouds perspire salt spray
to scrub soot and reduce the clank of tools and crush
of earth underfoot.

the distant mark of a timeless civilisation
appropriated by those already forgotten
trapped between colours
reduced to sepia
a jutting outcrop of navy blooms
On the border between factory and field
green and grey
red a generation ago
thick with blood that pulsed
now blue

severed.

CLOCKING IN

A balloon hangs over a carriageway
on a September commute

hovering in a breezeless space
surrounded by direction.

Gold sinks between warehouse and home
suspended in hope at winter's border.

Clocking in

David Comes to Life

comes to life.

PHEASANT

Caught in the rhythm of country lanes by dawn.
Rapeseed is reduced to grey. Orbs of light float on
blackened hills, marking villages I avoid. Thought
broken only by the daring pheasants that leave the
hedgerows for the safety beyond the road; the grassy
embankment to the reservoir. It calls its peace, its
promise the bird's life is worth a gamble. I thought
suicide was a human concept, an illness only we
suffer. Does the natural world know of the sadness?
Does it feel this weight?

A693

The nauseating contingency - most unlikely
But most provoking.
We're different men, but I'm the same.
Sculpted by pressure, motivated by words
I hope my son never hears.

A machine built before our time we should
have checked for wear. Stripped it down to
Skeleton, oiled and replaced.

We maintained it, scraped the rust,
and kicked it when it slowed. I left it behind to tick,
only audible on turbulent mornings and early drives.

A ghost at my neck on the A693. Roadworks
or traffic collisions slowing the journey,
as if to warn me.

NO PLACE, PITY ME, WALLISH WALLS, ONCE BREWED/
TWICE BREWED

If the crown hangs heavy,
the flat cap is of osmium.
Razor blades line its woollen skin
a cubist masterpiece wrapping
the cranium. A sordid ceiling
of the masochist's cathedral.
Knuckles align with the rhythm
of the hills, masts and turbines
the extended fingers of our lads,
slowly drowning. Moulded by the air
stolen from a formative throat,
flesh scooped and discarded like the root vegetable.
Years pass as missed steps, plunging organs
to darkness. Cheeks leak copper,
soaked up by an untrained palette,
rinsed and cauterised with the cheapest spirit.
Holes in a tongue, over-flowing with two-pound pints
and words censor-free but for the lost footing of weakness.

SCUM

Judge Holden and three
Jacks to be cut
usurped the order to proclamations
of history — it's how it's always been.
Ivory knives scalped the vests
of the largest plague pit, dusted
them down and pumped shit into their systems —
SCUM TAX scratched on the invoice.
Generation [insert] should see compensation.
For now, the notice is a measure too extreme,
industrial action a beacon for tabloid torture —
bastard wasps to something sweet.
The Derruti t-shirt and Goldman quotes are packed
away come Monday — I'm not afraid of ruins
but unemployment is something different.
Low-emission zones are nice,
but so are mandatory Eco-funerals
for the billionaires,
enforced by stripped fossil fuel
licenses and arse-slapping taxes.

I'm sorry, Sir. If you don't have an Eco-service, we'll be forced to
sink your yacht.

But I'm not dead yet.

I'm sorry, Sir, that's not my fucking problem.

PARTS, DEPARTED

It began in an age of weeping stars
of days owned by a bold sun unafraid
to cower and play host to cold days.

If stars wept today, we'd shoot them
from the sky with bullets made
for the skulls of boys, like those freshly growing
from the riverbed, as the sun's display
of strength reduces water levels to reveal
the murdered of a century ago – a family can rest
three generations later, knowing of his place.
He was never old enough to know his place
nor see the world without its smoke and hate.
Those lads' first taste of culture was a man
from a different country in a trench the same as theirs.
Those lads' first taste of culture, they were forced to hold a gun to.

The same burden of men still oversees a world
on fire and infinite war by bullet or bank.
Never enough to teach them to read
but plenty to produce arms to shoot the illiterate
and stage a heist – the crown needs new jewels, after all.
Never enough to get them a home
but plenty to celebrate the existence of a man and all his homes.
Oh, celebrate the legacy of an Empire conquered on oceans of blood.
Oh, how the brutes needed educating on the ways of the god-
fearing Englishman

Oh, God demands we bring civility to their lands.
If they disagree be sure to mutilate their headless corpses
to ensure no others follow. But teach the English children
of the Vikings and the Romans, the bastards who invaded
with nothing but violence on their minds.
Oh, the heathens.

Teach them how we gifted industry to the world:
the railways
and the bible
and literature
and politics
and equality.
Everyone can thrive, given they look like us.
Anyone else brings doubt to trust –
what will the foreigner with a tool do
to the nobleman with nothing but gunpowder and ranged weaponry?
Force King and God upon his people then perhaps we can trust him,
or the very least convince him our enemies are now his.

The tree of Empire,
its roots in every pocket and branches tapping at every door
the family forged by the Industrial Revolution, cast
in gold in the post-war West like a trophy
of failures to come: the father a breadwinner,
a suited ghost of the office, accessorised
by oversized glasses and computers
whilst the mother fed the children
a boy and girl,
he to haunt the office and she to raise her children

a boy and girl,

he to haunt the office and she to raise her children

a boy and girl,

he to haunt the office and she to raise her children

a boy and girl

he to hang himself and her to cry

how she didn't realise he was sad. She raises her children

a boy and girl,

to be open and honest

he to be told to man up and she to be labelled a hormonal, crazy ex.

A binary plague

he or she

and working or lazy

and lawful or scum

and happy or attention-seeking

and happy or silent

and happy or weak

and happy or …

and happy or …

After the trauma came the wave of self-violence,

the war no peace treaty could ever finalise.

Not even paid fairly for the self-hatred –

though if they down tools the walls of it all cannot be built.

And now the pacifists scream for civil war.

They're selling kidneys in shoe-boxes

from car boot sale pitches,

ID swiped from stacked wallets,

smokes lifted from corpses.

They're sucking the marrow from the bone
without a pause to save taste.

What will be left but the police and their pistols?
The politicians?
hidden away in third-home stables?
The bankers?
locked behind bomb-proof foyers?
The president?
assault rifle held high at the school gates with the troubled white man,
corrupted by [insert sub-culture death cult]?

Where does the tattoo ink go when we die?
The art embedded by compass needles,
every line another vein of our history
that they cannot wear, unlike the threads
pulled from funeral gowns, draped around sculptured necks
and threaded with teeth for jewels –
syllables of lost words caught in molar cavities where fillings once slept.
The only words to make the escape of wrought iron.
For we all know iron sharpens iron
and each quip is more deadly than the last.
Swilled away with the cheapest booze,
or thrown into a group chat for a glimmer of personality.

When the walls of it all begin
to crumble, who do you think they'll save:
the people or the product?

LAY OUT YOUR UNREST